THE BRACKEN ROAD
A Collection of Poems 2001-2021

by Brian J. Easley

DORRANCE
PUBLISHING CO
EST. 1920
PITTSBURGH, PENNSYLVANIA 15238

Dorrance Publishing Co
585 Alpha Drive
Pittsburgh, PA 15238
Visit our website at *www.dorrancebookstore.com*

ISBN: 979-8-8852-7309-1
eISBN: 979-8-8852-7443-2

THE BRACKEN ROAD

A Collection of Poems 2001-2021

Table of Contents

1
Avoidance

after everything you've done,
and after everything you've learned,
you still, after all this time,
allow yourself to be used and hurt by them.
you still trust them.
and even though they mean well,
they will pick away at you
piece by piece
until you're nothing,
until you're used up,
broken and poor,
until all your hopes and dreams have been dashed,
until you're just like them.
you must leave,
for your own good.
this isn't about being selfish;
this is about you seeing a problem, and avoiding disaster.

2
Warmth

as i sat there, hollow thoughts came flooding,
forcing memories out of darkness that had been buried.
i became a river,
and remorse left me for a moment,
replaced by hate and pain,
a newfound ally i wanted to nourish
because it felt so nice to be warm again,
so nice to feel something other than the cold;
other than complete sorrow and despair.
fists clenched, i stood in defiance,
but no one was there to meet me.
i was alone once again,
and the hurt poured forth into the nothingness
with an indeterminant volume,
and i drowned in it,
and with arms spread, i floated out,
finally content with it all.

3
A World Undesirable

so many dreams
i have to act, to teach, to learn,
all of which i fear will never come to light.
logic and reason simply seem to prevent
their existence or involvement in my life,
however unfair that may seem.
i can't see past them;
reality blinds me like the sun.
to be at the bottom,
the mundane world at my beckoning whim,
but who would want this?
a world undesirable,
a world unfit for one with dreams,
or is the point to escape that world,
so my children never have to experience what i have?
how unfair is life?
how trivial and wrong?
why must i continue the way i do,
alone and in pain,
tired and scared,
unsure of which road to take?
without a guide or path, walking blind,
surviving on a faith that seems to have left me.

4
Searching

searching for a bit of truth here in the dark,
my hands still don't work.
i'm still alone here in this place, and still without you.
i've kept all your letters;
they keep me company sometimes.
could it be after all this time, i still shudder at the way you were treated?
i still turn cold at myself;
i still hurt.
the shame, i fear, will kill me someday.
the truth stares me in the face and laughs.
i will never have you,
that you will never be mine again,
but sense says, "keep going, live your life,"
when the whole time i want to hear none of it,
having almost died without you.
a new taste for life seems bitter now at the realization you are missing
and have been.
only now i truly feel the void the quiet emptiness fills my soul.
and despite my best efforts to be happy and glad to be living,
my heart tells my head that my body can't work
without you near me.
you once told me that if you had a flower,
one little flower for every time you thought of me,
you could walk in your garden forever.
i often think of this in difficult times
and find i am the one walking through that garden,
for my thoughts are always with you.
every day, you pass by me in my mind,
and each day, your words seem clearer than before.
i haven't seen your face in years;
years without beauty,

without grace,
without love,
and that is what you are to me.
you encompass all which is good and kind and beautiful.
i am lost without you.
i have walked aimlessly with reckless
abandon,
searching for something that i ran away from years ago.
you are perfect to me,
and all in my life will seem dull and grey
since they in no way compare to you.
and i will suffer for it until the day i die, alone
still searching, for you.

5
Without Her

starting over again,
this time for sure.
can't live like this;
no, not anymore.
constant reflection,
can't not look back,
but now must go forward;
you've got to react
to a world without her,
void of peace and of hope.
missing that love and laughter,
her heart had been broke,
never not knowing
which turn you must take;
now that you're without her,
such a sad mistake.

6
Continued Despair

i meant what i said, you know,
when i said i love you still,
and everything and everyone won't ever know
how i feel except for you.
you once were the one for me,
and i you,
but now there is another,
and i stay here, holding true.
i mock the idea that we cannot reconcile the past.
though things will never be the same,
you must know i still love you.
you are the only one who i could talk to,
confide in,
and to this day,
you are the only one i want to spend my life with,
give my all to.
and though you will marry this man,
i will always remain yours
through war, peace, pain,
love, loss, regret,
push and shove.
never forget that i will never forgive myself,
and i will take to my grave all the pain which i caused,
all the hurt that i laid down on you,
all the questioning and insincerity,
the lack of trust and hope.
you are happy now, which is why i stay away,
why i stand clear.
i will never cause you harm again;
never be the source of your pain.
i cry because of this;

this hurts me more than any wound.
it is self-inflicted, this loathing,
and will forever remain so.
i will move on with my half-life
and experience life anew,
but without you here,
it all will be pointless.
Simply going through the motions will keep you alive,
but it will bring no meaning, no truth;
only continued despair,
only continued despair.
i don't want to live this way anymore;
i want to move on,
but i cannot shake your memory,
no matter my efforts,
for you occupy my every thought and will continue to do so
until the end of it all.

7
Tears

there are tears in my eyes tonight
that came from i know not where.
they will not stop,
won't disappear.
no matter how i hard i fight,
the emotion is too sharp;
now the memory is too clear
how i lost it all and you as well.
you have vanished into the crowd.
i feel as if i've died,
and the world beneath
has crumbled and wasted away.
my hope has left me;
the light has gone out.
love, please come back!
i'm writing this in the dark.
rescue this man!
i find a way outside;
the rain has started falling,
and it's followed by an awful gloom.
i'm too weak to help it,
too down to get up.
who will carry me?
there's no hope here;
none is left for us.
we are all gone;
we are all gone,
and i've lost my will.
it is nothing without you,
as i am.

8
Dependence

no matter how much we see the world change around us,
there are some who don't hear the call;
don't make the change.
these people are left behind by most
since they are too caught up in their own pasts,
too proud and sentimental
to move forward, press on with their lives.
these things have to be overcome,
these weaknesses;
these inadequacies;
these insecurities.
so many are left behind.
they will never understand the world unfolding before them.
the dark ages will fill them,
and they will become dependent on their failure;
on their fear to adapt to new circumstances,
to new life,
which springs up all around them
on all sides, unknown, complex, difficult.
and one who was once confident in himself is now just a child
looking out onto a vast jungle of life,
scared there may not be a path
away from his lonely valley
and hacking out one of his own is too horrible a thought to fathom.

9
Better Now

was i even ever good to you?
did i even ever try
to tell you how much i cared for you?
did i ever tell you why?
is there really a "too late"?
is that something you believe,
that there's no hope for another chance?
a way to show you that i see,
see how damn wrong i was?
see how it should've been to go back a few years?
see that i'm a better man.

10
Desert

it's getting quiet now, baby.
quiet thoughts fill the loud air,
thoughts about you and of yesterday.
yesterday's life wasn't fair.
i wonder now, what would happen
if you knew i had changed?
could you maybe love me like you did back then?
the desert is so lonely;
the mountains have all turned red,
a beautiful red in a desolate sky.
why must something so beautiful be so all alone?
i hurt when i think of you.

11
Love Song

i can never go home again,
can't go home and see my friends.
wanna know why?
cos you might be there,
and i'm scared of that,
cos if i saw you again,
i might fall once more for a girl who hates me…
is this a love song?
is this a love song?
i don't want to remember,
remember who i was,
remember what i was,
and what i ran away from.
what was i thinking?
is this a love song?

12

Get Away from Me

this place is different now
since you've gone so far away,
and it's not like you left me;
that's just what I need to say
to convince myself into thinking
i didn't treat you wrong,
and i didn't run away
from all i used to be.
or did i run from my youth?
i can't remember anymore…
yeah, right; i know it all,
and what i was back then,
what i had become…
the only way to change was to get out,
get out and get away from me,
who i was.

13
A Soldier's Composure

15

give me a reason, damn it,
to lose my composure.
go ahead now,
make me feel bad.
go on and try to hurt me,
cos i don't give a damn.
compared to you,
compared to you,
compared to you
i'm a better man.
if you want, you can order me.
if you want, you can order me.
just know i'm on edge here,
and i'm likely to lose it all.

14
Credibility

you must think i care or something
about your credibility,
cos you keep telling all these stories,
and they don't mean a thing to me.
you must think you're very special
since you can brag about yourself to everyone;
you seem to think you know
you aren't very impressing.
what is it you want to say this time?
how do i know it's not important?
aside to make you feel good about yourself,
how damn selfish can you be?
listen to yourself.

15
Forgive Me

what has happened here?
why won't you disappear from my heart,
from my head?
i tried to leave it alone;
i tried to move on.
but i know now what i was,
and i realize what i did.
i just want to make it up to you;
i just want to make it up to you too bad.
i know how you feel,
know that you don't want to talk to me,
know that you don't ever want to see me again.
where are all my friends now?
i wonder what they might think.
no way they're not mad at me for leaving;
for leaving,
i hope they know i'm better now,
that i'm sorry for how i used to be.
it wasn't your fault that i left;
there're other reasons too deep to bring back.
forgive me, forgive me.

16
Quiet

i don't know why i'm so quiet;
haven't figured that one out yet.
and i don't know why i can't talk;
no, not even to my friends.
why on earth am i so closed off?
why can't i let them in?
i want to breathe again;
i want to fly again.
i want to feel you.
if only i could tell you.
i need to show the world,
show them the reasons why i've become so quiet,
so very quiet.
you know i was different;
yeah, you remember me.

17
Normal

i don't want to be normal anymore
even though it's what i'm supposed to be.
i have to leave this place;
there's nothing here for me.
all this trivial shit is just too much,
and i just want to be free.
i need to be in a better place,
a place where i can grow.
i'm a better man now;
or at least i want to be.
i just thought you should know.

18
Looking Back

how does one reconcile a problem he started?
and is forgiveness something he should attain?
or is he supposed to learn his lesson forever?
and could she ever find a reason to return?
to forgive?
to love?

19
Discovery

i can't stand myself anymore;
it's time to make a change,
cos what the hell'd i leave you for?
i don't even know my own face;
my name doesn't match it.
they both seem broken and faded.
wish i could tell you how i feel.
it's been too long, you know,
and even though it seems so long.
i never managed to heal.
my life became so cold.
it's time to let it go—
runaway,
leave this place.
you've got to start again,
cos you can't keep living your life this way,
this way,
you need to find yourself.

20
Your Name

do these words mean anything all,
these words i've penned?
sentences among paragraphs,
what do you think, my friend?
are they worth the read?
i just can't seem
to get my point across,
or maybe i can.
we'll see.
i just can't stand all the
pain and loss some know.
i don't know what to make of this;
i can't even write your name.
i don't know what to make of this,
cos the truth is i'm ashamed
of myself, of my life, and the memory.

21
Grey

what on earth is wrong with me?
i have to get away
forgive me, release me.
do you remember the way it used to be?
fade away
into the grey,
the fine line where we all hide,
escaping our realities, escaping our calamities.
where on earth have i gone to i feel so far away?
far from you, far from me.
do you remember seventeen?
forgive me,
release me.
fade away into the grey, please don't…

22

Ghost

here i am, once again closed off another day.
my mind isn't blank anymore;
i can never get away
from the pain of this life and all the strife
that exists in this world between me and the girl.
she haunts my memory like an unrelenting ghost;
this isn't real.
i forgot how to feel, so cold now.
i'm afraid, so cold now.
i've become so cold.

23
A Little Crush

so, you had a crush.
a little infatuation.
and now here we are in the same situation.
all your friends keep telling me this,
but you say nothing.
i can't get you out of my head.
can i please say something?
why won't you speak to me,
and how come you're so scared?
if there was ever anything wrong,
you should know i'd be there
for you.
i'd be there for you.

24
Sunday

so i'll call you up on a sunday,
the last day i'm in town.
maybe we'll have a drink or two;
maybe we'll mess around.
and all your friends could giggle
about the fact that you went out
with some random guy.
and as for me and that random thing,
i guess it takes away the sting.
i guess i'll never know why you felt the way you did,
the way you do.
i'll return it;
i said i'll return it.
if you'd like, i'll give you all i have,
all i am,
and all i'll ever be.

25
Missing

could you be wondering how much i miss
my home, the memories, the places, and all the faces?
all seem to be so far gone.
my recollections aren't the best,
but if they serve me right,
you once kissed me 'neath the old oak tree
where we watched the stars at night.
only a few things move me when thinking of home;
you always seem to be among them.
what am i supposed to do?
move on?
let the memory die?
the truth is, i'm missing home so badly that anything,
oh, anything, brings me back makes me happy;
makes me whole again.
so thank you for giving me something to smile about
even though i know you don't feel the same.

26
Hint

why can't i think any happy thoughts?
all i feel is pain.
i know they are there,
floating, falling
as thoughts often do
somewhere in my mind
as a reminder happiness exists,
but for some reason,
that's all those thoughts are:
reminders.
the hint is there, but they are so faint now,
they only linger.
they never stay, never stay.

27
Closure

closure is a word i use
when thinking of the old days.
it was something i needed,
something i needed,
something i wanted in my life so torn.
you were the seamstress who put me back together.
you were the one who set me right
when i went wrong right,
when i was wrong;
i went so wrong,
and all the problems i was trying to solve and bring closure to
blew back in my face.
i was such a disgrace, i couldn't face you;
not like that.
i was weak when i should've been strong
for you,
for me,
for all that we should've been;
all that we should've become.
closure became a word synonymous with losing you,
for when i labored so hard
to fix the situation i was in,
i drifted,
drifted so far away from you,
yet i took control of my life and the things happening to me.
i began to realize
what i needed to do,
the man i needed to be.
i solved my stupid problems,
or at least learned to deal.
now i'm sitting alone thinking about the way
things could have been
and the way we were.

28
Intention

in my mind, i'd seen you before;
you're all i know.
and my dreams, i cannot ignore
the feelings that show.
did you walk away intent on coming back?
or were you simply too tired of all the painful thoughts and feelings between us
that i had acquired?

29
Closer

oftentimes i lay in bed looking up at the ceiling,
listening to music that somehow made it into my life
while i was consumed by your memory.
and every lyric to every line speaks to me more now than it did before,
and every thought of every moment i spent with you hurts so bad,
i can't ignore being alone just isn't what i want anymore.
i can't handle being without you, even though it's too late
at least i know that now.
at least i understand that i can't stand
being without you.
nothing can replace your face in my mind;
no rain, no wind, no pain can move that image.
my heart pours out onto the floor,
over and over again,
cos like a broken record,
my memories skip to that one moment when i lost you,
lost you forever; this is killing me.
you were all i ever had, and now i am nothing,
and everything means nothing,
and that nothing is all i have to replace you,
so i will embrace it
with every fiber of my being
if it brings me closer to you.

30
Progress

what is this world coming to
if we can't even see the truth,
if we can't even see the use
that comes with abuses from all the truces
that others all seem to confuse?
believing in something that's right is all that i want to do,
and if you can't understand my mind,
why should i even give you a clue?
why should i bother when somebody offers to sell me a total lie?
is it my compassion or failure to ration out?
why i would even reply?
and would she believe me if i was completely honest in telling her why
believing in something that's right is all that i want to do?
and if you refuse to understand me,
what the hell else can i choose?
should i be disgusted to even have trusted someone who caused my pain?
or should i accept that it might be correct?
we're more different than we are the same.
why can't we start over?
honestly, tell me why.
can't you see we're all hurting here in some way?
what are we afraid of?
why won't we go forward?
so often, it seems hopeless.

31
Around

we sleep under the same sky,
but you don't know i'm looking.
we see with the same eyes,
but you think mine are closed.
what is there to create
when i can't even seem to feel?
all i can do is make-believe
our love is something that's real.
we talk to all the same people,
but they're your friends, not mine,
and they might even think i'm a fool.
but they don't know my mind.
when did this all happen?
when did i first believe?
why do i lie to myself, and why must i deceive?
i miss our talks that never happened,
and the love we never made.
i hurt to think we may have lasted to know my memory will fade.
and it will eventually;
i have to accept that.
i know, i know, i know, i know;
i must accept that.
but for now,
this place is so much better with you around.

32
Ducks

ducks in a row in step together,
never gonna grow; birds of a feather.
people get in line, look left, then right.
don't forget to wait your turn—
mustn't offend anyone tonight.
mustn't rock the boat.
no, no; we can't do that.
what would be the point of our fucking lives if we disappointed,
if we fell out?
never have i been so alone, so angry with the world.
saddened to see what's going on,
embarrassed i know them at all.
oh, no—can't be alone;
can't have different ideas.
have to follow the herd, the crowd.
if we don't, we're doomed.
they'll never leave you be;
they'll hurt you through and through,
take all you wished you'd ever known,
finish everything you'd want to do.
it will all mean nothing in the end,
remember that, remember,
and everything you thought to be the truth
from your life will all be severed.

33
Greed

walking forward, never ending,
can't move past it, keep pretending
we all want it, the pain we're sending to all of those not comprehending
because we know we're right;
maybe closed off and stubborn,
are we as worldly as we think?
should this be our concern?
who are we to decide the law of other lands?
if we were living over there, this would be on our hands,
and here we squabble over little things,
which don't mean much at all.
but over there, it's different, isn't it?
who are we to make the call?
we can't afford it;
our polls will drop;
our numbers and our stocks might flop.
yet it's our steadfast duty
to push ahead to the goal,
to sweep the truth under the rug,
to make the people fold.
and we don't want to plan ahead;
we don't want to succeed.
is it the money in the end?
is that all that we need?

34
Division

this place escapes me;
i can't figure it out.
who the hell was she,
and can i go without?
everything's changing,
so nothing is the same.
am i going crazy,
or is the world just insane?
can i keep going,
or should i turn around?
i've made it work so far,
though nothing has been found.
realize my mind here;
please realize my heart.
i have never left you;
we've simply grown apart.
and the ocean between us and the stars up above
can never part us.
they can't divide our love.

35
Seagulls

he lives with the seagulls now since she is long gone.
they wait around for him on sunday;
he doesn't know where they come from.
she is lost and gone forever,
and all he does is watch the weather,
for they won't ever be together.
with love, it's better now than never.
he knows the way the wind blows now,
they all seem to push him away
she used to breeze by him as they do,
but that was yesterday.
she is lost and gone…
…better now than never.
they met one night under the stars;
she told him of her love.
they held each other close that night,
but he wasn't who she was thinking of.
she is lost…
…better now than never,
he had a choice; could've said no;
went to the brink but just let go.
she is gone…
…better now than never.
and now she's with another whose love for her grows dim.
only now she will discover,
she lies down and thinks of him.
but he lives with the seagulls now
since she is lost and gone…
…better now than never…

36
Home

i think of my home
as a trampoline never jumped on,
covered in vines under a setting sun.
there's a beautiful garden with flowers,
and green surrounded by bricks that cross in between.
the windows are dirty, yet still under care,
my memories inside them with the love that's still there
i miss all my family;
i hope that they're well.
though i roam the world over,
in my heart, they will dwell.

37
Another

you've become someone i can't ignore,
a candy sweet memory from a life lived before.

38
Verily

40

stunningly glamorous,
shockingly scandalous,
beautifully, wonderfully, truthfully amorous.
loyally dutiful,
fully reputable,
physically, mentally, verily sensual.
you are to me one
who's now irreplaceable,
and i love you.

39
Over and Over

words adrift,
set ablaze by emotion all alone,
until set into motion, rounded up,
made up as a gift presented to you
in hopes they'll seal the rift.
never you mind reading them over and over.

40
Morning

something moves me by the way you enter the room;
it's something with the way you seem to float past everything.
there's a style and grace that i can't touch,
which leaves all else shining.
each morning i wake up to you right there next to me,
i can't help but be happy satisfied with life.
my love completes me;
and being whole is something that sets me free.
wherever you are, i want to be with you.
wherever you go, i have to go there, too.
whatever you want, i want to give it to you,
cos you have my heart, and i must follow.
i don't want it back, and i don't feel hollow;
it's safe with you, i know.
please keep it with you forever.
can we be alone, just one more time?
if we can't, i'll lose my mind,
cos you know that love's hard to find.
you can trust this;
you can love this;
you can keep this always.
you have my heart;
you have my soul.

41
Belief

give me something to believe in,
cos no one believes in me.
it'll give me something to hold onto,
a chance to focus my emotion.
my life as i once knew her is gone,
and i'm sitting here so all alone,
so the only thing keeping me from losing it all
is the idea that you might save me somehow.
tell me the truth,
if you could be there for me, i'd like to know the truth.
some truth would be nice,
some kindness could be good,
and goodness kind for me.

42
Burning Man

i thought we would go to war together,
but you just went home.
there's no comfort for me there
in that you feel nothing for me;
won't give yourself up to the idea.
why do i wait here,
cold, naked?
why do I stay here,
alone, fading?
the idea that there's more than this
hurts my soul,
makes me stay,
makes me feel.
you can't tell me this was for the best.
since you think me so naïve,
i will retire from this course
and make my feelings known.
i'll never be the same again;
i'll not say a word.
i am no longer one;
i only feel this place
as one without it can,
but it surrounds me,
preventing my escape.
my feelings warm to it,
seek to heal the frame,
but there's nothing for me;
there is nothing here—
only turning; turning over again.
where only i am burned,
i am the burning man in my dreams.

43
Mortimer Brown

he left the house at midnight and got into his car;
he drove for thirty minutes until he reached the bar,
and there he had a few drinks and bought a few for some.
the very men he once knew well from whom he could not run,
they talked about the old times, when mice and men were made,
and fondly recollected memories that would not fade.
he felt a mighty pain then
of temper and of doubt;
and though they warned against it,
he knew he must get out.
so building up his courage and fortifying strength,
he strode out of the back door and walked down to the lake.
he walked along the shore line;
he stumbled to and fro.
he knew there could be nowhere else,
nowhere else that he could go.
for the woman he had loved so dear had left him and was gone,
and everyone he knew and loved had used him like a pawn.
he sprinted down the dock then and hopped into a boat,
and at half past two that very night, he slit his bloody throat.

44
Lonely

alone again,
but this is new to me;
you were so right,
so right.
the slightest hint
of things going wrong,
not what i wanted,
not right starting again;
i'm so good at it.
not something to brag about, alright?
here alone, here again by myself,
thinking about you, about it all.
can't get it right, can't think tonight,
won't sleep; nightmares are there, waiting
for me to arrive:
tossing, turning, growing uncomfortable.
pondering on something, would it have worked?
yes, i think so,
but working,
this is something
i don't want to have to do.

45
Familiar

you look like someone,
but i can't place the name or name the place
where i would've known you.
why is it you are so familiar?
i've never spoken to you before this moment.
something in your eyes is calming, settling my fears
that you might not be interested if i spoke to you.
your smile might forgive the fact that i don't know what to say to you;
your hands might comfort a place in me that can't be comforted.
where have i heard this before?
maybe it was when i first saw you,
somewhere in my dreams.

46
Reality

she was given wings so early in life,
simple security is all they offered;
secure in life,
the future ahead,
waiting to be grasped,
pinned down
earlier than most.
no shelter
is all he ever had;
working every day,
future uncertain,
waiting to spit on him.
what in common,
if nothing at all,
that they were in love insignificant.
she'd not support him;
his dignified pride,
he'd not hurt her.
her beautiful naïveté,
they'd live on love?
an impossibility!
so it was over all over now.
they traded something:
he had her wings to fly from her;
she had his pain to haunt her.
now,
the world keeps them apart,
along with their dispositions.

47
Unintended

this isn't what i wanted;
i thought that you should know,
cause everything i'd hoped for
left me so long ago.
all of this is foreign;
this life, this place, this hour.
and everyone i thought i knew all want to see me cower,
down,
down on my knees,
simply unable to rise.
i am frozen these days from wearing my disguise;
this road to nowhere,
i've been on so long;
every inch of every turn
so far has all been wrong,
destined to make the same mistake again, again, and over,
a realization that couldn't convince you;
couldn't say i never loved her.
these days, i am so tired
of all the same decay,
and turning over a new leaf just might be in store today.

48
Never

the never, as you put it, is all around me now;
the never has taken hold,
and though i'm free of you,
the never has taken hold.
it grips me like a fever;
it screams; it won't let go.
and though i fall in deeper,
the never won't let go.
the never, as i know it, has taken me to friend;
the never isn't lonely; the never's not a trend.
the always is where you are so happy and so sweet;
the always is so comforting to you and not to me.
the never's where you'll find me,
though you will never look,
for i should be too far gone,
like a chess board and the rook:
always on the outside,
moving forward all the time,
never turning,
always churning,
and the never is my queen.

49
JazzBlues

listening to the calming coolness of the blues,
or to a symphony in the form of jazz satisfies to the fullest hilt.
my journey for contentment, my quest for self,
it is only for a moment.
the dream is conjured, but it lasts forever,
the memory of the cool the idea of the calm,
the slow-moving pace,
rhythm,
the mood permeates my soul.
my being is formed into another
with the sax, the drums, the trumpet;
their feelings, emotions, hopes.
they become my own;
i am born anew,
am whole again.
at least until the next note,
the next phrase,
the next song the next life.

50
Reflection

anyway,
like i said before,
he's all wrong for you.
he rants,
he curses,
he raves on and on,
just like me.
anyhow,
like you know,
he's so bad for you.
he cheats,
he lies,
he takes on and on
from you, like me,
and so what now?
like i told you once before, it should be over.
right now; for real; forever.
then again,
he means well.
he wants to change…
no; nevermind.
he talks to himself, too critical
of world, of life, of self.
what does he have to say for himself?
nothing.
nothing at all…figures.
people in the mirror only say what you want them to.

51
Into the Woods

into the woods we go again,
can't stop this time; can't slow down.
we might not make it, got to make it on time;
just got to keep moving! didn't come to quit.
not our mission—maybe yours; not mine.
never was mine. it just happened only once.
didn't see the point; didn't care.
know better now; know better this time.
can't quit;
not again.
never was a good loser; never suited me.
nothing much did back then, only did it because it was easier;
always with the easy way out, always the easy way.
least resistance, least resistance; not ready for it, for you,
for anything—
responsibility, accountability, resounding quiet;
always resounding quiet.
the words, not there; emotion either.
feeling escaped with them, truth purged from life
by none other; swept away by none other; hidden
by none other hiding;
gone from me into the woods.

52
Brother

i always wanted to fly.
you see, to be alone and above,
to be seen but remain untouched beyond harm,
beyond fear flying, soaring
so like an eagle above all the rest,
making up for things left forgotten,
heading for a new life.
out past the horizon, wherever the rainbow ends,
there, we'll start over.
i hope to see you there wherever the rainbow ends.
i always wanted to be remembered as the one who made it,
not the one who fell behind, crippled by the world
and everything it did to us.
i never saw it coming;
never heard the shot
that brought us down to earth,
to the land that time forgot.
we were happy once, weren't we?
happy to be apart,
happy to be together,
happy to have this heart,
flying above the rest,
no longer grounded helpless,
wherever the rainbow began.

53
Thunder

wishing she was here with me,
even though we've never met,
hoping one day that she might see
that i'm not all that bad,
wanting so badly for her to know
that i'm someone who could be worth wanting as well.
just as well,
i thought might as well never know,
might lose that focus which got me here;
that focus which, in the end,
is utterly meaningless without someone like her
 whom i've never met except in my mind,
in my imagination.
i suppose i'll hear thunder
the first time she speaks to me.

54
The Return

coming home, returning,
it all comes back full circle,
memories like rain pouring down,
pouring out.
looking in the mirror,
not liking what i see,
talking to old friends stories differ between.
everything is changing
but has always stayed the same
coming home,
returning,
it all comes back, back to me,
full circle.
memories like voices screaming out
from within,
churning the past long forgotten,
remembering now, remembering how, remembering why
i left in the first place.

55
Hell

another one gone, another one lost,
that's what i keep hearing;
another one taken,
another one shot,
another one's not leaving.
give me a reason why,
come on, tell the truth.
something other than your fucking lies just might have to do
because another one's gone,
another one's lost,
another one wasn't looking
because you set us down into a fucking nightmare.
now my friend's not coming home;
my brother, my sister,
not coming home.
never coming home again to see the lights,
to see the friends
and all the opportunities you've taken,
horded for yourself,
kept for your own,
the elite mind;
the collective peace collected for a price
that some stupid poor kid had to get for you,
so you could sit around on your sorry ass
and watch it all on tv.
freedom this freedom that;
the only freedom i'll ever know
is six feet fucking under
your lies,
your contempt,
your condescension, your insecurity,
and your goddamned greed.
i'll see you down there,
where all the others are waiting.

56
Life

beginning again from the beginning
is much harder than i thought it'd be.
so much is new;
so much has changed,
and i'm not ahead of the game at all.
did i lie to myself?
was i too naïve?
is everything a show, just like i was afraid of,
just like i thought it would be?
but what if i don't make it?
i at least have to try,
because no one will help me, not ever;
not in this life.
nothing will be handed down, given, or delivered.
there is no foundation
to which i might be tethered;
no guiding light
other than my own soul, my own.
none other than my own.

57
Maybe

alone again;
another saturday night on my own again
by my own design.
is it my fault i push them all away?
is it my fault i'm never here to stay?
is it my fault i play the games i play?
yes and no.
yes and no;
yes and no
come round once more.
can't ever let it go.
i'm found once more;
we've done this all before.
is it my fault i push them all away?
is it my fault i'm never here to stay?
is it my fault i play the games i play?
yes and no.
yes and no;
yes and no,
and now we're here together,
and all this time has passed.
i warned you what would happen,
but you never cared to ask
why it went on this way.
you were happy with the past;
maybe that's what did it.
could i have met my match?
could we belong together,
and could you be the cure
for all my past transgressions against all those before?
and even though you love me,

and you know i do too,
i hope i never fall back into the lies that seemed so true.
is it my fault i push them all away?
is it my fault that i play the games i play?
is it my fault that i'm never here to stay?
yes and no.
baby, yes and no;
x and o.
yes and no;
alone again,
another saturday night on my own again,
and it's by my own design.

58
Bridge

when burning your bridges…
be sure not to strand yourself…

59
Yours

62

everything up to now
everything has been set up for you,
either by yourself or by others;
others who may love you or hate you,
and a few who think they love but who's only purpose in life is to ensure your demise.
now,
what to do? change yourself
as so not to be led astray or destroyed by anyone.
you've had your whole life to prepare;
you've had your whole life,
your whole life your life,
yours.
yours and yours alone.

60
3 AM

it's 3 am;
i can't sleep again;
thinking of you keeps me up at night, i suppose.
lying here,
eyes wide open, holding on to nothing,
wishing it was you.
focus on the dark
all around,
calling your name
and not hearing a sound. so alone…
could you be, too?
thinking of me, uncomfortable,
kicking the sheets;
cold and then warm,
reaching for me,
being held in my arms,
rolling in bed,
pillow held tight;
wish it was me holding you tonight.
my thoughts are drifting;
there's only your face,
a vision to me turning to a dream.
clouded now
as you disappear into the morning,
falling asleep again.
hope i think of you,
hope i see you there in all of my dreams.

61
Relative Comfort

uncomfortable in his own skin; infallible.
thought he was again forgivable,
wishes he could be noticeable,
just wants her to see.

something changed in him when he looked into the mirror;
something hurt inside.
he'd realized he was without her.

recoverable,
this love it is not discoverable.
a new line of thought impenetrable.
her heart had come to be sufferable;
his life would forever be.

something changed in him when he looked into the past;
something hurt inside.
his regret had come at last.

uncomfortable in his own skin.

62
Withheld

a decision had been made,
a certain point reached;
the point of no return
a life would be left behind and memories allowed;
a long-awaited chance to burn his mind was fading.
the lights had grown dim;
she knew what she had to do.
the pain was draining
the sight of him.
there was nothing left to prove.
all alone,
he made the journey
so far along the broken path,
and all in all,
he knew her yearning
to look at him and try to laugh,
but she could only cry.
and she could only cry;
held back tears for so long,
held back her tears for so damn long.

63
Promise

coming apart,
seams undone,
cursed once again to tread this path.
alone once more,
stoic at best,
not sure of what's to come.
the lie had been told;
the stage set
for another to come
unwound, unkept.
a promise would be broken;
a life shattered.
for all that was once above him now didn't matter.
he thought about forgiving,
about taking it all back,
but hindsight means
we don't get a second chance
to change the things we would.

64
Name

67

what's in a name?
they say a memory,
a reputation, a life;
a lie.
what's in a name?
they say a question,
an answer.
you toss the die.
what's in a name is what i hate about myself,
about this life set up for failure.
crippled for life,
what does it matter?
start anew,
start again;
easy for you,
so easy to say that no one knows,
do they?
do they want to understand?
is it easier to shun?
do they feel better about themselves?
it's hard for me:
nowhere to begin;
nothing to hold on to;
no way to push off anymore.

65
Ledge

i was born in the cold february
and set upon the ledge.
my mother said, "hang on";
my father just smiled.
shivering and hungry,
i did my best;
my brother was there,
my sister as well,
straining for grip;
position;
relative comfort.
we learned along the way,
during our time at the edge.
we learned to look up;
we learned to look down.
the people above,
the people below,
all smiling,
confusing me.
both seemed welcoming,
as much as they could be
without outstretched arms;
arms meant to hold, pull, catch even.
the ones above,
too high to bend down and take my hand;
the ones below,
too far down to land safely upon.
my father fell;
my mother, my brother, my sister…
what was i to do?
after all,

wasn't i here for a reason?
i couldn't just fall.
wasn't i here for a purpose?
to catch them as they fell;
to pull them up if they made it this high?
i'm getting tired of this ledge,
this edge, this middle;
this buffer between high and low,
rich and poor,
good and bad,
healthy and sick…
i'm getting so tired of simply holding on;
I don't know
How much longer can I keep this hold,
this grip,
this moment.
someone help me up!
please,
i confess
i do not want to fall!
i do not want to lose this grip
and be caught
below the ledge.

66
A Jig of Us

i would bleed for you
and you don't care.
that's not part of your story,
your poem, your song;
the one you set the beat of your life to;
the rhythm of your heart.
set to the tune of pain, hurt, and regret,
you'd like a fucking jig to dance to
that reminds you of us
and the times we had,
which would then lead you
to the recollection
of how you ended it all
and destroyed us,
just so you could have some goddamned drama in your so-called life.
love isn't truth nowadays;
the sad, fucked-up story we tell afterwards is what we want;
that reminder of how cruel we were
and how small we made someone feel,
so we'll never do it again.
all part of some fucking soap opera
you did not warn me you were into.

67
Fair

it isn't fair; it isn't fair
the way that she moves,
the way she moves me,
and it's not right.
it isn't right; it isn't right
the way she loves me,
the way she loves.
we started to sing together until we were torn apart;
we wanted it to be forever.
should have known it from the start, and it's not cool
with me
the way she left and what she said.
it's not a sweet taste in my mouth.
it isn't fair
the way she tempts me towards the edge of sanity, and it's so sad.
it's so sad.
the reflection in the mirror, he stares at me.
his hollow eyes, those hollow eyes,
they tear at me; they tear away
everything i used to be, and it's a change,
the way i feel today,
now that i know she's gone and she'll never be with me,
she'll never be with me.

68
Steppingstones

i'm broke down, tired, and alone;
i feel like i haven't got a home,
and i think i'm finally ready
to go on with my life,
cos' i haven't felt steady,
and i haven't felt right.
i'm done now, and able to keep on.
i'm finished with always being wrong.
i feel like you should know me
the way i want to be and not how i remember
the things i guess you've seen.
i'm broke down, tired, and alone
since we broke up last night over the phone.
i wish that i could replay
the things that i don't like
and everything i screamed to you from my motorbike.
i'm drunk now; heavy, and obscure.
i'm alive, but i couldn't be for sure.
and you are gone, and i have changed,
but it's too late to rearrange
the steppingstones;
they all have been erased.
the steppingstones,
they all have been erased.
the steppingstones, they all have been erased.
the steppingstones, they all have been erased.

69
On Flying

73

vast fields of white,
billowing plains of airy foam;
how you remind me of the open sea.
silently, you stretch across the sky,
interrupted only by storms conjured by the gods.
dear sun, open a path for me in those darkened skies
that i may see my home once more.

70
Montauk

74

driving out from the city,
careening through the hamlets and hamptons out to montauk
to see the lighthouse;
washington's dedicated pillar,
which provided safe passage
to those crippled by night, fog, and stormy sea for so many years.
if only i could provide that service;
give that gift
if only to one person,
i suppose i could claim a small victory in my life,
knowing i had steered you clear of the rocks, dear friend.

71
Cowardly Lion

your jowls beckon me near in curiosity
then beat me back with cruel ferocity.
i, too, am an animal
and have the capability you do
to warn, intimidate, and awe
with adorning might and grace.
perhaps we will meet again,
the outcome different than it were
in this life.
i, too, am uncontrollable;
we are equals at least in that.
too strong for each other,
cancelling out all compromise,
pushing and pulling for position,
a sexual dance of power.
the schism between us,
between two animals,
cold and strong,
selfish and loud.
i, too, am powerful.
hear this animal roar
with indecisive intention
to keep you underneath me,
just as you would do
if i were weaker.
we only succeed in failure
beneath the deafening roar.

72
My Lover's Ghost

twenty times she told me,
twenty times and then
some more for good measure.
an enlightening push,
a stormy nudge
right to the edge of clarity.
she never once asked me
what i thought i felt.
she never once asked me
what i could have done.
every night, she showed me
what she wanted me for,
and every time i knew it.
i chose to forget,
forgot her touch,
a warm let down;
engaging glances
gathered around.
she never once asked me
what i needed most.
she never once questioned
my lover's ghost.
what could i say?
every night, another story.
where did she go,
and who told her
about the truth?
the truth behind
my lover's ghost.

73
Never Again

i'm in no position to start over,
in no position to begin again.
and with little motivation,
i've ensured my own demise
but i would much rather fail
than spend one more minute
under her heel,
under her.
she makes my life uneasy,
makes my spirit waiver,
makes my heart ache
for the romance we once had
before reality set in,
before we were ambushed.
lovers no more,
a continent apart
and angry.
never again,
never again
that touch;
the brush of skin on skin;
his beard across her neck.
and the tension,
at first polite and childish,
then new and daring,
then intense and full of power,
that tension that is now unbearable.
rude and cruel,
a rough tension
that rings truer to the definition.
he cares not for the fight,

the competition.
he only wanted his lover back,
his friend,
and the promise that they once held;
the ideal dream-like love
that he should have known
couldn't exist with her.
the memory will bury him,
just as they buried their love
under a mountain of lies and deceit,
the grave marker misplaced.
never again
a lover's touch,
a friend's embrace,
never again.

75
Peter Miniscule

miniscule, they called him,
not worth a second glance.
in fact, it should be his last name—
peter miniscule:
no higher than a child,
which is what he was;
just a poor child,
undeserving of their taunting,
"but someday," he said.
"someday what? you'll be shorter?"
"no," he said, "someday."
and that was all he needed;
the strength to carry on.
they pushed him on monday,
 spit on him the next;
scuffled and huffled and tripped him
as wednesday and thursday went by.
friday was the worst;
a punch for each breath after school near the park.
his way home, always blocked
by those who didn't know him;
those who hadn't a clue
what he would become,
whom he would be
to them—to everyone.
the years went on. "peter miniscule!
at your service," he said mockingly,
his wit in good form;
his intellect sharp from all the beatings.
his mind was a magnet
if information was metallic,

and he clung to it all.
nothing could satisfy
his need to fulfill
the space left in one's life
when you can't go outside,
the fear almost as great
as the passion that replaced it,
eventually catching up
in height with the rest.
he left them behind;
did great things, never looking back
or feeling sorry for himself.
thinking back couldn't help anything, nor anyone.
they were wrong; that's that!
revenge is for the close-minded, the jaded.
he would place himself above it all,
above what anyone else would do,
for he was peter miniscule,
the enlightened,
the righteous,
the philosopher-king.
and no one would ever treat him that way again,
and he would never do the same,
no matter the memory,
no matter the pain.

75
Claire

she sings almost too well, moving us all.
the notes too perfect; guitar under her spell,
she sees me in front in her line of sight,
connecting for a moment, the world seems alright.
but you don't know me; never met before.
how could we connect when i feel like a bore?
i swear i won't blow it;
please, give me one chance to show you i'm worthy
of your song and your dance.

am i just another someone along for the ride of your life?
god i hope not;
that would be more than i could handle,
more than i could enter into.
god, please,
everything i want to be,
let her see it.

her glance, too engaging;
i stir in my seat,
hoping to god that the look was for me.
i almost stand for her to show that i know,
but where would that get me?
i'd ruin the show.
she slows down her strumming and begins to cry;
the song she is singing brings tears to her eye.
and just as she ends it, she looks out at me.
a smile cracks from under the sad reverie.

was i just another simple sam
along for the days of your lives?

god, i do hope not.
i hope it was real.
these feelings i'm feeling are more than i can handle,
more than i'm equipped for to deal,
god, please,
everything i'm going to be,
let her see it;
let her see it in me.

76
A Return to Red Bricks

a return to red bricks makes me think of sleeping,
sleeping for years,
dreaming of a life
that i was throwing away.
walking the campus paths makes me shudder
at the years i stayed indoors;
the blood boils
when i think of the view from the tower,
a view i've never seen. the splendid skyline
of the county seat of bexar,
i did everything right this time and was still denied.
that chance, that absolution,
that chance, that redemption;
a way to prove i'm more than i seem.
never again will i return to those red bricks.

77
Second City

are you the second city because of fire or insecurity?
i've wondered this so long,
and now i find myself here,
thinking along the same lines. my life,
in shambles and ash,
came here to rebuild confidence and ego;
down in flames, reconstructing my life, beginning again.
so many times over, this feels normal,
however troubling, however unfair.
brought it upon myself once again.
love does that sometimes; love without a future.
could she really have been that shallow?
or was it just an illusion
of a great city skyline? built for me;
dead now, a scar on this horizon.
foundations the only remnants, rubble at my feet;
love at my feet,
lying there,
abandoned, charred and alone,
waiting for someone to come to care
to rebuild her.
love doesn't have to perish in fire.

78
Children of the Rifle

i grew up almost a mile from the rifle range.
day and night, I heard the shots;
rounds discharging,
imagining an explosion of light as they went,
spent casings plunging to the ground.
i can identify somewhat with children
from countries fraught with chaos and war,
imagining the same sounds outside of their windows
that i heard everyday:
bullets whizzing by;
bombs going off,
exploding in the night.
beirut, mogadishu, baghdad, saigon…
only a few of the places i imagined growing up,
hearing the violent bursts of battle
echoing outside my window,
but the only real chaos i experienced
along with most other people i knew
was inside the package of our latest video game;
was on the television every night;
or in the latest release i could catch at the movies.
never reality;
never real,
the staged retelling of something true.
i wept for those children then
when i realized they had the better deal, though most horrible.
at least they were living in the present;
the gritty, painful, awful truth of life,
not the glazed, glossy, reproduction of it.
i wept for them again
when i knew they might never see the end of it,

never feel the happiness i had,
never see the hope, or love, or friendship
that I was born into.
the plague was on them,
and the only way to get them out,
the only way to set them free,
is to grow up and invade;
invade their lives and let them out
of their cage, of their prison.
i may have had the rifle range,
but what is that compared to reality?
in the end, nothing…

79
Hungry

you've never known
what it's like
to be hungry,
and you've never known
what it's like
to be afraid
that tomorrow
might not come around.
you've never heard
the wolves howling
on the wind;
to hear them circling,
circling round your cold bones.
and you've never felt
the sun bearing down,
walking alone through it all
with nothing
but you love the songs
and all the singers
who claim to know it,
all when they only know
what it's like
to be wanted.
they'd do whatever it takes
to get a message across to you,
and all that they say
and all that they are
and all that they do
means nothing compared to my love.

80
Expensive

when you tell me
you're expensive
it makes me wonder why,
why i would want someone
or something
that's for sale
when i don't want
to have to buy your love?
when you don't tell me
that you love me
or want me back,
it makes me wonder
why i even talk to you at all.
why would i torture myself
over someone
or something
that doesn't want me?
when nonchalance
is your game,
i'm forced to think
that whether you won't admit it
or secretly long for it,
something is going on with you,
and you want someone else.
why would i want to be with someone
who doesn't give me the time of day?
who positions and lies,
keeping everyone on the line,
acting as false as her intentions,
living in her lies
and believing they're true?

you're not expensive;
you're just lost.
and you've lost the value
of what love could really be:
more than money;
material wants;
a shallow expression of affection
that i refuse to give,
will not sign on for.
love should be so much more
than a business arrangement;
love is so much more
than business.

81
Lottery

imagine your life
after the lotto.
think about what it would mean
to your family and friends
if you won that game.
think of the deeds to be done,
the wrongs corrected,
the realities possible.
imagine the shock,
the absolute joy,
which occurs at that moment
when the numbers match.
the mouth opens;
the breath retreats;
eyes water;
a scream emerges;
or possibly fainting to the floor
is far more likely.
travel
to the end of debt
and the beginning of comfort and security
for you and yours.
is that worth the gamble,
the one dollar one forks over
at that one in a million chance
at a new life,
a new start,
a new everything?

82
October

sitting alone,
listening
to it all.
a life gone by,
asking myself,
why wait?
why stand idle?
lying here,
doing nothing?
with what do i go with
when i have nothing?
only bitter memories
of a life gone by.
learning from my mistakes
and preparing
for the ones ahead,
i see them so clear.
ahead on the horizon,
turning north
to the cold chill
of the future,
the metropolis of the real.
the hand of god,
lift me up
to the place
and the life
that i deserve;
the life
that should have been.
i'll wait for you there
in that city
instead of waiting
for no one here.

83
Highway

driving towards a new life,
heading north
thinking 'bout the old life
and what the hell it was worth,
everything that led to me
being here.
driving alone
in the cold,
freezing rain
blurring my vision
of the landmarks and road signs
parallel to my life.
the good and bad;
the ugly and sad
guiding the way,
fueling the light.
lovers gone and buried,
lying on the roadside;
families torn apart;
people laid asunder,
swept beneath my wheels…
always swept beneath these wheels.

84
Chicagoland

the exciting feeling rushes over me
driving through downtown
on my way home
towards my new home.
chicagoland calling me
from wherever i may be.
chicagoland calling me,
soon i'll be home free.
a vibrant chill of the cold
as i stop in for a drink
in old town,
paintings on the walls
celebrating another life;
so many other lives
all entwined around us.
chicagoland calling me
from wherever i may be.
chicagoland calling me,
soon i'll be home free;
soon we'll all be home free.

85
Raincheck

i was sad when i missed you tonight,
but it just couldn't be helped.
i'm not there right now;
i'm so far away.
it's hard to live
when i'm caught this way,
like a chain around my leg
pulling another life along
when i just want to be alone with you,
just for a little while,
long enough to show you
i'm not completely gone,
not so far gone
that i can't love someone,
let someone in

86
Revision

95

i'm writing again,
trying once again
to begin this life;
creating something
a little bit at a time,
hoping inspiration finds me
at least before famine
can track me down
and hold me accountable
for the things i've done.
but life is only known
to those on the bottom.
real life in the world
is the person who was never knocked down
without an opportunity to get back up;
real life is known to those who are born there
at the bottom,
churning under the feet of society,
succumbing to the tide,
falling behind the rest of us,
always in the back;
pitiful cries all round.

87
Elevator

my life changed that day
riding up the elevator
all the way to the fifth floor.
it was like taking a lift to heaven.
the second great depression
had been averted.
crying as i ascended,
sobbing as i thought of the past few days.
life had thrown a curve,
and i wasn't ready;
almost starving,
asking for help
from whoever knew me well enough to decipher my pleas.
i'm an enigma in that way:
maybe too proud,
perhaps too strong
for my own good.
a little humility,
a bit of truth
remind us that we only have so much.
life lets us know sometimes,
lets us know we need help;
that we're only human,
and those of you without everything
know this to be true.
my life changed that day in the elevator
when i got that check in the mail.
i learned one of the hardest lessons
that no one should ever have to learn.
crying in the elevator
on my way to heaven,
on my way to life.

88
Dresser Drawer

97

i'm not gonna ask you where i went wrong;
i'm not even gonna say his name.
and if this is the way you treat the ones you love,
i'd love to see how you treat the ones you hate.
like mcclure said,
there's a diamond ring
in the top drawer of my dresser.

89
Comal Trilogy
Part I: Bracken

in the distance, like a castle,
cement plant dominates the horizon,
owned the skyline
other than trees and lights

the cops from garden ridge would follow him home,
whether through bracken or down the lane.
winding down marbach or the straight bindseil shot
got him home in time to see the sunset through the windowpane.

eighty-one-eighty, that was the address.
used to tell his friends his father built that home with his bare hands,
but in reality was just a cheap lot in the woods,
and he knew the contractor

on occasion, they'd go into bracken,
which wasn't much unincorporated lives,
outside of any order
countless votes to stay independent or stay a backwater.

he broke his finger setting pins at the bowling alley;
he loved the burgers at the general store;
got his truck worked on there at the collision center,
and his father drank beer at the hangin' tree saloon.

used to go to parties at the volunteer fire station
before it moved and the nonsense village popped up nearby,
touting the wares and spoils of wealthy neighbors;
a sideshow of what could have been.

too often, little, tiny towns get ignored, and things pop up nearby,
looking for the same character, but never succeeding,
becoming just another attempt at some kitschy mall;
someplace some rich guy's wife can sell the crap she made while bored.

90
Trade

i would trade anything
to see your smile once again.

trade a house
i don't own;
trade a car got on loan;
fifty dollars in my bank;
a motorcycle
that wouldn't crank.

seven dollars in my hand;
trade a beach full of sand;
trade a mountain that I drew;
trade a kite that we flew.

trade my wallet,
trade my heart, trade my fate,
trade my part,
trade my shoes full of holes,
trade my shirt;
pearl snaps are gone.

trade my family,
trade my name,
trade my feelings—
hurts all the same.

i would trade anything
to see your smile once again,
to see your smile once again,

91
With You, With Me

with you, i'm stuck out in the rain;
with you, i'm feelin' only pain.
with you, i don't want to hear your name
cos i've just gone and done it to myself again.
i've just gone and done it to myself again.

with you, i could do mighty things;
with you, the hurt didn't seem to sting.
with you, i never needed a ring,
and i've just gone and done it to myself again.
i've just gone and done it to myself again.

with me, you had a greatest fan;
with me, you had more a drunk than a man.
with me, you never really gave a damn,
and you don't need that shit in your life no more.
and you don't need that shit in your life anymore.

92
Wasted

wasted hours,
wasted days,
ways of thinking,
ways to change.

wasted feelings,
wasted pain,
wasted drinking,
wasted fame.

wasted dollars,
wasted change;
ways of being,
these days are strange.

wasted lovers
in my heart;
wasted devils
gave my start.

wasted friendship, loud and clear;
wasted fortune
through the years.

wasted future,
wasted past,
wasted beer
in my glass.

wasted time,
wasted space,
wasted body,
wasted face.

93
Songbird

she's a songbird
in my hand,
singing things
i can't understand.

she is perfect,
she is grace;
she ain't here
in this place.

she is gone;
ain't comin' back.
makes me feel
like i'm gonna crack

she's a songbird
in my hands,
singing things
i can't understand.

oh, oh, oh, oh.

she is money;
she is fame.
she is torture;
she is shame.

she is lovely;
she is the sun.
she is painful;
she ain't no fun.

she's a songbird
in my hand,
singing things
i can't understand.

she is never;
she is none
she is everything
and everyone.

she's a songbird
in my hand,
singing things
i can't understand.

94
Alone Again

out a window from the library,
lookin' for you
cos you ain't
lookin' for me.

squirrel comin' down
from the tree;
parking lots are all empty.
the parking lots are all empty.

i believe in things
that maybe you don't;
i believe that life
is kind of a joke.

i think my mind
is darker than most,
but that don't mean that i'm not in love with you;
that don't mean that i can't love.

our love has been something from a dream,
if a dream was the same as a nightmare.
i mean the longest night
through which i couldn't sleep.

i don't think that i can sleep again with you;
i know that i can never go to sleep.

skies are full
of clouds that are grey.

lighting comes
along with the rain.

i ain't scared,
just a little bit afraid.
all I know is that i'm alone again;
all I know is that i'm alone.

95
Up The Valley

she said she'd come up the valley,
she said she'd come up the valley,
she said she'd come up the valley,
she said she'd come up the valley.

she said she'd know when the time was,
she said she'd know when the time was,
she said she'd know when the time was,
she said she'd know when the time was.

said she'd love to meet the family,
said she'd love to meet the family,
said she'd love to meet the family,
said she'd love to meet the family.

where'd she go, knows nobody,
when'd she go, knows nobody,
where'd she go, knows nobody,
where'd she go, knows nobody.

cos I never saw her pretty eyes;
i never heard a last goodbye.
i never knew the reason why
i didn't see her up the valley.

i never knew the smoothest skin;
i couldn't believe that i couldn't win.
i couldn't guess where she had been;
i didn't see her up the valley.

i just need to know when'd she come up the valley,
when'd she come up the valley,
when'd she come up the valley,
when'd she come up the valley

and they found her down the valley,
they found her down the valley,
they found her down the valley
they found her down in the valley.

Drums

109

i wish the drums played all night long, all night long
all night long;
i wish the drums played all night long, all night long
all night long.

i wish the drums
played all the way home, all the way home
all the way home.
i wish the drums
played all the way home, all the way home
all the way home.

97
Wishin'

wishin',
i am wishin'.
thinkin',
i am thinkin'.

bleedin',
she was bleedin'.
sinkin',
we were sinkin'.

lovin',
i was lovin'…
nothin'
apparently.

livin',
we stopped livin'.
feelin'
left suddenly.

losin',
i'm always losin'
everythin'
she gave to me.

98
Wealthy

wealthy in my years,
wealthy in my years,
tried to hide those tears,
what she usually hears.

poverty is here;
have another beer.
forget all your fear;
drive home—crash—scream—steer.

cry about his jeers;
try to hold her near.
too late to revere;
everyone just leers.

99
Diamond

so you went home,
and i moved out;
felt alright
to be out on the ground.

got a diamond ring
in my dresser drawer;
it don't mean a thing,
not anymore.

you came home,
and you broke down
cos i wasn't there;
couldn't be found.

furniture gone,
keys on the floor,
you grabbed your phone
and went for the door.

called out my name
across the phone
i answered, "hey,"
like i had before.

"where did you go
and why did you leave?"
"cos you asked me to;
couldn't live with me."

"was just trying to
get you to agree
that you had become
a broken man."

i had become
a broken man.

got a diamond ring
in my dresser drawer;
it don't mean a thing,
not anymore

it's too late now;
already gone.
shouldn't have known;
it's in plenty of songs.

that when a broken man,
doesn't get along,
might as well just let him go;
might as well just let him go.

got a diamond ring
in my dresser drawer;
it don't mean a thing,
not anymore.

100
Late

I am too late,
I am too late.

101
Violins

violins are playing,
trying to hear
what they're saying

102
Field

running through the field,
i feel my hands around the neck of all that's real.
i can't seem to get around it;
the only one to see it wasn't all i need.
it wasn't for the field to be reaped;
farmer got his name
from leaving it the hell alone.
i can't take all the blame
for being the only one who didn't speak your name
like it was the greatest ever.
the joke is, it's a shame
that everyone thought so highly of her.
it was all her game,
and then maybe not even that much.

www.ingramcontent.com/pod-product-compliance
Lightning Source LLC
Chambersburg PA
CBHW052047150726

48002CB00002B/785